WHO AM I?

Preschool Workbook B

WHO AM I?

Preschool Workbook B

Second Edition

First Edition Authors

Mary Jo Smith and Jerelyn Helmberger

Revision Author

Mary Jo Smith

*Educational
and
Theological Advisors*

Most Rev. John M. LeVoir
Mary Jo Smith

IMAGE OF GOD SERIES

IMAGE OF GOD, INC., CRYSTAL, MN
IGNATIUS PRESS   SAN FRANCISCO

Nihil obstat: Reverend Joseph Johnson
                   Censor Librorum

Imprimatur: ✠ Most Reverend John C. Nienstedt
                   Archbishop of St. Paul and Minneapolis
                   May 10, 2012

For teacher information go to www.ipreligioused.com

Cover design by Riz Boncan Marsella
Cover and text illustrations by Barbara Harasyn

2022 reprint
First Edition published 1991 by Ignatius Press, San Francisco
Second Edition published 2012 by Ignatius Press, San Francisco
© 2014 by Image of God, Inc., Crystal, MN
All rights reserved
ISBN: 978-1-58617-370-8
Printed by Friesens Corporation in Altona, MB, Canada on March 2022
Job Number 283308
In compliance with the Consumer Protection Safety Act, 2008

CONTENTS

LETTER TO PARENTS OR GUARDIANS

Dear Parents or Guardians,

This year your child will be using the "Who Am I?" preschool curriculum from the *Image of God* series. This series is centered on the subjective turn found in the writings and teachings of Saint John Paul II. This subjective turn stresses the dignity of each individual as a person made in the image of God. Because we are images of God we possess a great dignity. This also means that the better we know God, the better we will know ourselves. Your child will more deeply come to understand this through studying this curriculum.

The preschool program has as its focus two key ideas: God and creation. These key ideas, along with an emphasis on Sacred Scripture, form the unifying element of the lessons.

You, as parents or guardians, are the primary religious educators of your children. With this in mind, the "Who Am I?" curriculum has take-home materials which provide a basis for faith discussions at home with your child. There is a set of worksheets for most lessons. Sometimes your child will bring home a completed worksheet to share. Sometimes, though, it will be up to you, as parents, to complete the worksheet with your child.

On the back of the worksheets you will find Family Notes. These contain the Scripture reference for the lesson's Bible story, which has been adapted for children; an explanation of the main focus of the lesson, providing you with background to discuss the lesson with your child; the concept of faith that was the foundation of the lesson, presented in a question-and-answer format; a Correspondence to the *Catechism of the Catholic Church* section that lists the topics taught in the lesson and that provides references to the corresponding paragraphs in the *Catechism of the Catholic Church*; and a suggested home activity for you and your child.

It is our hope that through this program you and your child will grow in faith together.

Directions: Cut out the boxes. Glue one box in each leaf.

God the Father	God the Son	God the Holy Spirit

Family Note

Lesson 1: There Is One God—The Blessed Trinity

In this lesson, the Sign of the Cross and the Glory Be are introduced. Each time we make the Sign of the Cross, we give praise to the three persons of the Blessed Trinity. When we say the Glory Be, we are showing that we believe that God always was and always will be.

Concepts of Faith

How many Gods are there?
There is one God, and there are three persons in the one God: Father, Son, and Holy Spirit.

What do we call the three persons in one God?
We call the three persons in one God the Blessed Trinity.

Correspondence to the *Catechism of the Catholic Church*

Belief in one God: *CCC* 199–202, 228
The implications of faith in one God: *CCC* 222–27, 229
"In the name of the Father and of the Son and of the Holy Spirit": *CCC* 232–37, 265
The revelation of God as the Blessed Trinity: *CCC* 238–48, 261–64
Blessed Trinity in the teaching of the faith: *CCC* 249–56, 266
The divine works and the trinitarian missions: *CCC* 257–60, 267

Suggested Activity

Review the Sign of the Cross and the Glory Be with your child:

Glory be to the Father
and to the Son, and to the Holy Spirit,
as it was in the beginning, is now,
and ever shall be, world without end. Amen.

Directions: Connect the dots and color the picture.

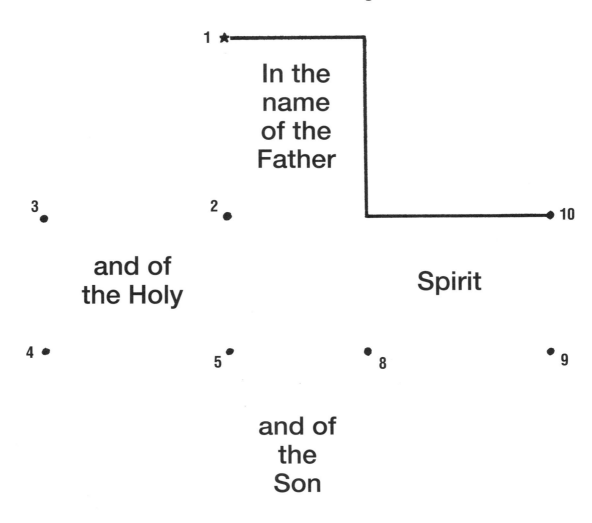

1 ★

In the
name
of the
Father

3 •

2 •

and of
the Holy

Spirit

4 •

5 •

8 •

9 •

and of
the
Son

6 •

7 •

Family Note

Lesson 1: There Is One God—The Blessed Trinity

In this lesson, the Sign of the Cross and the Glory Be are introduced. Each time we make the Sign of the Cross, we give praise to the three persons of the Blessed Trinity. When we say the Glory Be, we are showing that we believe that God always was and always will be.

Concepts of Faith

How many Gods are there?
There is one God, and there are three persons in the one God: Father, Son, and Holy Spirit.

What do we call the three persons in one God?
We call the three persons in one God the Blessed Trinity.

Correspondence to the *Catechism of the Catholic Church*

Belief in one God: *CCC* 199–202, 228
The implications of faith in one God: *CCC* 222–27, 229
"In the name of the Father and of the Son and of the Holy Spirit": *CCC* 232–37, 265
The revelation of God as the Blessed Trinity: *CCC* 238–48, 261–64
Blessed Trinity in the teaching of the faith: *CCC* 249–56, 266
The divine works and the trinitarian missions: *CCC* 257–60, 267

Suggested Activity

Review the Sign of the Cross and the Glory Be with your child:

*Glory be to the Father
and to the Son, and to the Holy Spirit,
as it was in the beginning, is now,
and ever shall be, world without end. Amen.*

Directions: Circle the things God has made.

God made the whole world and everything in it.

Family Note

Lesson 2: We See God in the World around Us—Creation

The story for this lesson is an adaptation of Genesis 1:1–31. We call God Creator because he made the world and everything in it from nothing. God made all the things in the world for people to use. We can use all the things God made, but we cannot use other people. We love, praise, and thank God for the wonderful world he has given us.

Concepts of Faith

Who made the world and everything in it?
God made the world and everything in it.

Who is our Creator?
God is our Creator.

Correspondence to the *Catechism of the Catholic Church*

The Creator: *CCC* 279–81
Catechesis on creation: *CCC* 282–89
The world was created for the glory of God: *CCC* 293–94, 319
The mystery of creation: *CCC* 295–301, 317–18, 320
Man created in the image of God: *CCC* 355–57, 380–81

Suggested Activity

Go for a walk with your child. Point out all the wonderful things God has given us.

Creation Booklet

God made the sun, moon, and stars.

God made the plants and trees.

Family Note

Lesson 2: We See God in the World around Us—Creation

The story for this lesson is an adaptation of Genesis 1:1–31. We call God Creator because he made the world and everything in it from nothing. God made all the things in the world for people to use. We can use all the things God made, but we cannot use other people. We love, praise, and thank God for the wonderful world he has given us.

Concepts of Faith

Who made the world and everything in it?
God made the world and everything in it.

Who is our Creator?
God is our Creator.

Correspondence to the *Catechism of the Catholic Church*

The Creator: *CCC* 279–81
Catechesis on creation: *CCC* 282–89
The world was created for the glory of God: *CCC* 293–94, 319
The mystery of creation: *CCC* 295–301, 317–18, 320
Man created in the image of God: *CCC* 355–57, 380–81

Suggested Activity

Go for a walk with your child. Point out all the wonderful things God has given us.

Creation Booklet

God made all creatures great and small.

God made Adam and Eve in his image.

Directions: Find and color the hidden animals.

Adam and Eve named the animals.

Family Note

Lesson 3: I Am Special to God, Who Made Me

The story for this lesson is an adaptation of Genesis 1:26 and Genesis 2:18–23. We are all special because we are images of God. We can love and act the way God loves and acts. We can share God's life. As images of God, we want to teach others about God and his love for us. The good things we think, and say, and do help others see and learn about God through us.

Concepts of Faith

Why are we special to God?
We are special because we are made in the image of God.

Correspondence to the *Catechism of the Catholic Church*

Man created in the image of God: *CCC* 355–57, 380–81
Equality and difference willed by God: *CCC* 369

Suggested Activity

Together, look at pictures of your child as a baby. Discuss how much your child has grown.

Directions: Circle the things animals can do.

**Animals cannot act as images of God.
Only persons are made in the image of God.**

Family Note

Lesson 3: I Am Special to God, Who Made Me

The story for this lesson is an adaptation of Genesis 1:26 and Genesis 2:18–23. We are all special because we are images of God. We can love and act the way God loves and acts. We can share God's life. As images of God, we want to teach others about God and his love for us. The good things we think, and say, and do help others see and learn about God through us.

Concepts of Faith

Why are we special to God?

We are special because we are made in the image of God.

Correspondence to the *Catechism of the Catholic Church*

Man created in the image of God: *CCC* 355–57, 380–81
Equality and difference willed by God: *CCC* 369

Suggested Activity

Together, look at pictures of your child as a baby. Discuss how much your child has grown.

Directions: Help Moses climb the mountain.

God gave Moses the Ten Commandments.

Family Note

Lesson 4: Actions and Attitudes—The Ten Commandments

The story for this lesson is an adaptation of Exodus 20:1–17. God gave us the Ten Commandments to help us know how to live as his images. They are a way of life for an image of God. The Commandments are not rules or laws forced on us, but rather the way an image of God chooses to act. When we choose to act as an image of God by following the Commandments, we show our love for God.

Concepts of Faith

How should we show our love for God?
We should show our love for God by choosing to follow the Commandments that he gave us.

Correspondence to the *Catechism of the Catholic Church*

The Old Law: *CCC* 1962
The Ten Commandments: *CCC* 2054–69

Suggested Activity

Work together with your child on a small project or task. Have your child help you make a cake, wash the car, set the table, make a bed, etc. Point out the steps or directions you follow to do this project or task the correct way.

Directions: Connect the lines and color the tablets.

THE TEN COMMANDMENTS

Family Note

Lesson 4: Actions and Attitudes—The Ten Commandments

The story for this lesson is an adaptation of Exodus 20:1–17. God gave us the Ten Commandments to help us know how to live as his images. They are a way of life for an image of God. The Commandments are not rules or laws forced on us, but rather the way an image of God chooses to act. When we choose to act as an image of God by following the Commandments, we show our love for God.

Concepts of Faith

How should we show our love for God?
We should show our love for God by choosing to follow the Commandments that he gave us.

Correspondence to the *Catechism of the Catholic Church*

The Old Law: *CCC* 1962
The Ten Commandments: *CCC* 2054–69

Suggested Activity

Work together with your child on a small project or task. Have your child help you make a cake, wash the car, set the table, make a bed, etc. Point out the steps or directions you follow to do this project or task the correct way.

Directions: Cut out the pictures. Put them in the correct order.

Family Note

Lesson 5: Love Others as God Loves You

The story for this lesson is an adaptation of Luke 10:30–37. We are made in the image of God to do what God does. God loves us; God loves everyone. This means that because God loves us and everyone, we should love ourselves and everyone else. First we should love God, then we should love ourselves, and then we should love others as God loves us. When we love others, we make ourselves happy because we are acting as God made us to act.

Concepts of Faith

Whom does God love?
God loves everyone.

Whom are we to love?
We are to love God, ourselves, and everyone else.

Correspondence to the *Catechism of the Catholic Church*

God, "He Who Is", is Truth and Love: *CCC* 214, 231
God is Love: *CCC* 221, 231
The Holy Spirit—God's gift: *CCC* 733
Communion in spiritual goods: *CCC* 952
Marriage in God's plan: *CCC* 1602
"Male and Female He Created Them": *CCC* 2331
Holy Orders: *CCC* 1593–98
The communal character of the human vocations: *CCC* 1878
The Christian family: *CCC* 2204–6
Conversion and society: *CCC* 1889

Suggested Activity

Give your child an extra hug. Say, "I love you."

Directions: *Match the action to the place.*

We show our love for God in different ways.

Family Note

Lesson 5: Love Others as God Loves You

The story for this lesson is an adaptation of Luke 10:30–37. We are made in the image of God to do what God does. God loves us; God loves everyone. This means that because God loves us and everyone, we should love ourselves and everyone else. First we should love God, then we should love ourselves, and then we should love others as God loves us. When we love others, we make ourselves happy because we are acting as God made us to act.

Concepts of Faith

Whom does God love?

God loves everyone.

Whom are we to love?

We are to love God, ourselves, and everyone else.

Correspondence to the *Catechism of the Catholic Church*

God, "He Who Is", is Truth and Love: *CCC* 214, 231
God is Love: *CCC* 221, 231
The Holy Spirit—God's gift: *CCC* 733
Communion in spiritual goods: *CCC* 952
Marriage in God's plan: *CCC* 1602
"Male and Female He Created Them": *CCC* 2331
Holy Orders: *CCC* 1593–98
The communal character of the human vocations: *CCC* 1878
The Christian family: *CCC* 2204–6
Conversion and society: *CCC* 1889

Suggested Activity

Give your child an extra hug. Say, "I love you."

Directions: Circle the items we see in God's house.

A church is God's house on earth.

Family Note

Lesson 6: God's House—The Church

Through this lesson, the children should come to respect the items found in the church and come to know the correct behavior for church. God's house is a place of prayer and celebration. Mass is our most important prayer. At Mass, stories about God are read, and at Communion, God gives us the gift of himself. Sitting quietly and listening to the stories about God, saying prayers, singing the songs, and showing respect for the things found in God's house can be gifts of love offered to God. We should be careful with the books and other things we see in church. We should remember that God is in church with us in a very special way.

Concepts of Faith

What is God's house on earth called?
God's house on earth is called a church.

Correspondence to the *Catechism of the Catholic Church*

Three degrees of the Sacrament of Holy Orders: *CCC 1554–71*
The Sacrament of the Eucharist: *CCC 1324–27*
What is this sacrament called?: *CCC 1328–32*
The Eucharist in the economy of salvation: *CCC 1337–44*
The movement of the celebration: *CCC 1348–55*
Names and images of the Church: *CCC 751–52*
Characteristics of the people of God: *CCC 782*
Christ is the head of this body: *CCC 792*
The Church is one, holy, Catholic, and apostolic: *CCC 811*
The Church is apostolic: *CCC 857–60*
The bishops—successors of the Apostles: *CCC 861–63*

Suggested Activity

Visit your parish church when there are no services. Let your child walk around the church looking at the statues, stained glass windows, etc.

Directions: Cut out the figures of the children. Put them in the pew.

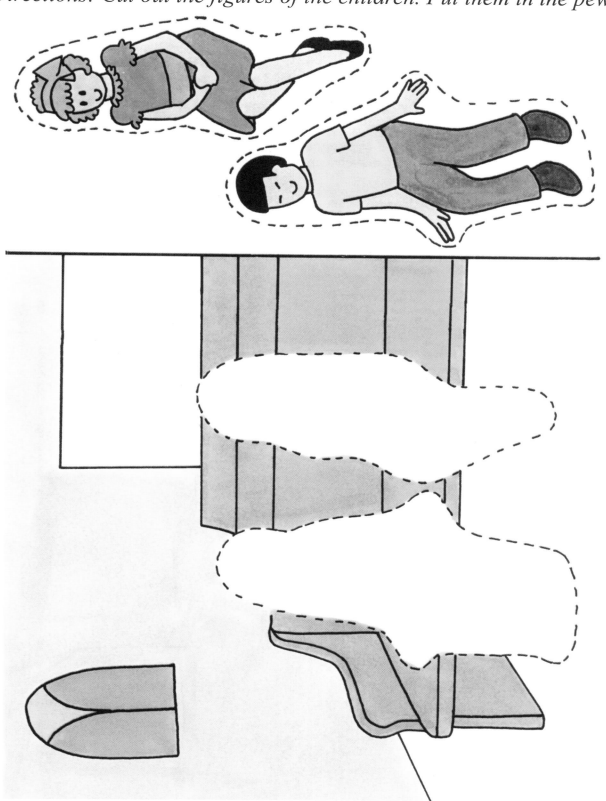

We sit quietly in church.

Family Note

Lesson 6: God's House—The Church

Through this lesson, the children should come to respect the items found in the church and come to know the correct behavior for church. God's house is a place of prayer and celebration. Mass is our most important prayer. At Mass, stories about God are read, and at Communion, God gives us the gift of himself. Sitting quietly and listening to the stories about God, saying prayers, singing the songs, and showing respect for the things found in God's house can be gifts of love offered to God. We should be careful with the books and other things we see in church. We should remember that God is in church with us in a very special way.

Concepts of Faith

What is God's house on earth called?

God's house on earth is called a church.

Correspondence to the *Catechism of the Catholic Church*

Three degrees of the Sacrament of Holy Orders: *CCC* 1554–71
The Sacrament of the Eucharist: *CCC* 1324–27
What is this sacrament called?: *CCC* 1328–32
The Eucharist in the economy of salvation: *CCC* 1337–44
The movement of the celebration: *CCC* 1348–55
Names and images of the Church: *CCC* 751–52
Characteristics of the people of God: *CCC* 782
Christ is the head of this body: *CCC* 792
The Church is one, holy, Catholic, and apostolic: *CCC* 811
The Church is apostolic: *CCC* 857–60
The bishops—successors of the Apostles: *CCC* 861–63

Suggested Activity

Visit your parish church when there are no services. Let your child walk around the church looking at the statues, stained glass windows, etc.

Directions: Color the picture.

Adam and Eve disobeyed God.

Family Note

Lesson 7: Wrong Choices

The story for this lesson is an adaptation of Genesis 3:1–24. Even though most of the children are not of the age of reason and thus technically cannot sin, it is important to establish a sense of right and wrong. Along with this awareness of morality should come a sense of sorrow and a need for forgiveness when a wrong is committed. When we choose to do something we know is wrong, we are not clear images of God. We have displeased God. Sin is the opposite of love.

Concepts of Faith

What happens when we make a wrong choice?
When we make a wrong choice, we hurt ourselves, we hurt others, and we hurt God.

Correspondence to the *Catechism of the Catholic Church*

Consequences of Original Sin: *CCC* 55–58, 399–400, 402–9, 416–19
Obedience of faith: *CCC* 144–49
The Fall of man: *CCC* 385–90, 413
Man in paradise: 374–79, 384
Original Sin: *CCC* 388–90, 396–401, 415
Reality of sin: *CCC* 386–87, 413
The spirit of the promise: *CCC* 705
Man's freedom: *CCC* 1730–48
Promise of a Redeemer: *CCC* 410–12, 420–21

Suggested Activity

Let your child choose an appropriate snack to make as a surprise for the rest of the family.

Directions: Circle the tree that is different.

God said, "Do not eat from the tree of good and evil."

Family Note

Lesson 7: Wrong Choices

The story for this lesson is an adaptation of Genesis 3:1–24. Even though most of the children are not of the age of reason and thus technically cannot sin, it is important to establish a sense of right and wrong. Along with this awareness of morality should come a sense of sorrow and a need for forgiveness when a wrong is committed. When we choose to do something we know is wrong, we are not clear images of God. We have displeased God. Sin is the opposite of love.

Concepts of Faith

What happens when we make a wrong choice?
When we make a wrong choice, we hurt ourselves, we hurt others, and we hurt God.

Correspondence to the *Catechism of the Catholic Church*

Consequences of Original Sin: *CCC* 55–58, 399–400, 402–9, 416–19
Obedience of faith: *CCC* 144–49
The Fall of man: *CCC* 385–90, 413
Man in paradise: 374–79, 384
Original Sin: *CCC* 388–90, 396–401, 415
Reality of sin: *CCC* 386–87, 413
The spirit of the promise: *CCC* 705
Man's freedom: *CCC* 1730–48
Promise of a Redeemer: *CCC* 410–12, 420–21

Suggested Activity

Let your child choose an appropriate snack to make as a surprise for the rest of the family.

Directions: **Connect the lines and color the picture.**

God said, "This is my Son. He has pleased me."

Family Note

Lesson 8: God's Family—Baptism

The story for this lesson is an adaptation of Matthew 3:13–17. Baptism is the beginning and the foundation of our union with God. Through the Sacrament of Baptism, we receive the gift of grace. Grace is God's own life. Grace makes it possible for us to act as images of God and makes us members of God's family. Therefore, grace helps us get to heaven.

Concepts of Faith

Who are the members of God's family?
All baptized people are members of God's family.

What is grace?
Grace is the gift of God's own life that he shares with persons.

Correspondence to the *Catechism of the Catholic Church*

"In the name of the Father and of the Son and of the Holy Spirit": *CCC* 232–33
Sacraments: *CCC* 1113, 1131–34
Sacraments of Christ: *CCC* 1114–16
Sacraments of the Church: *CCC* 1117–21
Sacraments of faith: *CCC* 1122–29
Sacraments of salvation: *CCC* 1127–29
Sacraments of eternal life: *CCC* 1130
Baptism: *CCC* 1213–84

Suggested Activity

Together look at pictures from your child's Baptism. Discuss that special day.

Directions: Color the picture.

At Baptism, we become members of God's family.

Family Note

Lesson 8: God's Family—Baptism

The story for this lesson is an adaptation of Matthew 3:13–17. Baptism is the beginning and the foundation of our union with God. Through the Sacrament of Baptism, we receive the gift of grace. Grace is God's own life. Grace makes it possible for us to act as images of God and makes us members of God's family. Therefore, grace helps us get to heaven.

Concepts of Faith

Who are the members of God's family?
All baptized people are members of God's family.

What is grace?
Grace is the gift of God's own life that he shares with persons.

Correspondence to the *Catechism of the Catholic Church*

"In the name of the Father and of the Son and of the Holy Spirit": *CCC* 232–33
Sacraments: *CCC* 1113, 1131–34
Sacraments of Christ: *CCC* 1114–16
Sacraments of the Church: *CCC* 1117–21
Sacraments of faith: *CCC* 1122–29
Sacraments of salvation: *CCC* 1127–29
Sacraments of eternal life: *CCC* 1130
Baptism: *CCC* 1213–84

Suggested Activity

Together look at pictures from your child's Baptism. Discuss that special day.

Directions: Connect the lines and draw a picture of someone forgiving another person.

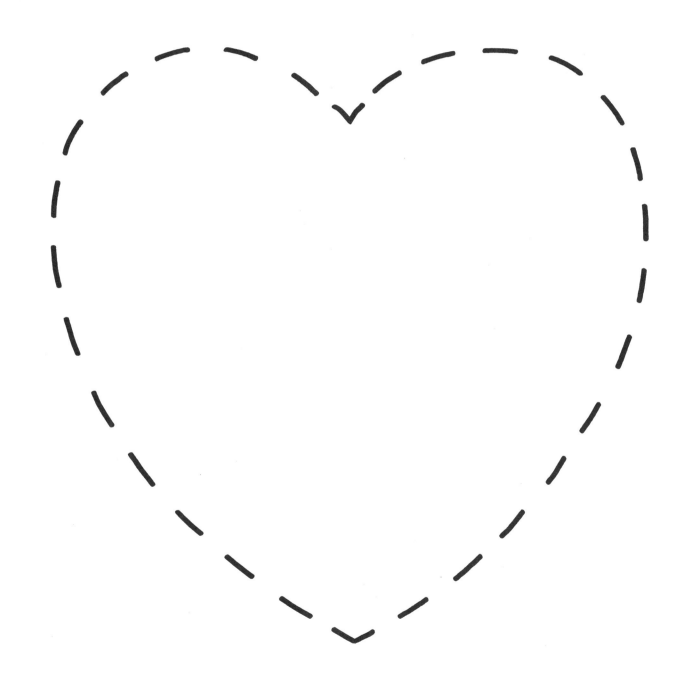

Forgiveness is an act of love.

Family Note

Lesson 9: Forgiveness Is an Act of Love

The story for this lesson is an adaptation of Matthew 18:21–35. It is important that the children understand that we all make wrong choices, sometimes causing hurt or unhappiness to others. This does not mean that we are bad persons, but rather that the deed is wrong and unacceptable to God. When we have done wrong, it does not mean that God and the person we have offended no longer love us, but rather that we have hurt them and need to ask for forgiveness. Saying "I'm sorry" is only half of asking for forgiveness. We must also show through our actions that we are truly sorry and will try to do better.

Concepts of Faith

Whom do we ask to forgive us when we do something wrong?

When we do something wrong, we ask God and the person we have hurt or disobeyed to forgive us.

How should we forgive others?

We should forgive others as God forgives us.

Correspondence to the *Catechism of the Catholic Church*

The Sacrament of Penance and Reconciliation: *CCC* 1440–45, 1487
The acts of the penitent: *CCC* 1450–53
Satisfaction: *CCC* 1459

Suggested Activity

Help your child say "I'm sorry" and ask forgiveness from someone who has been offended.

Directions: Draw a happy face and a sad face.

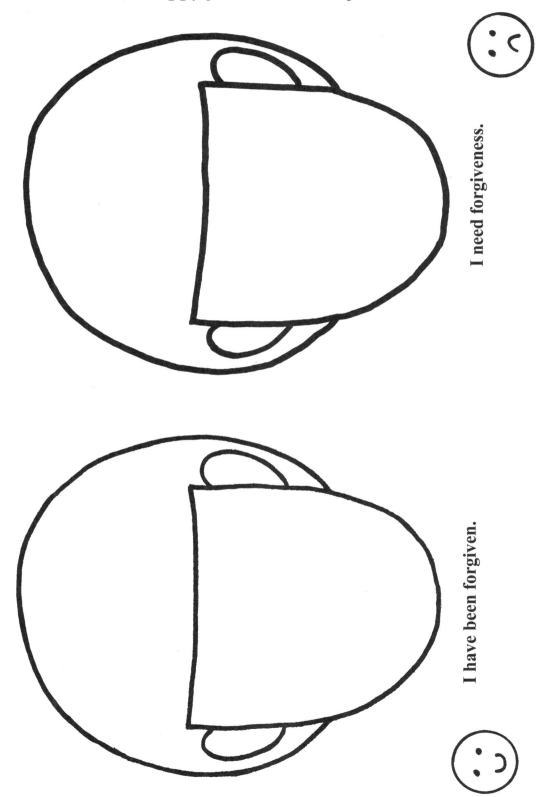

I need forgiveness.

I have been forgiven.

Forgive others as God forgives you.

Family Note

Lesson 9: Forgiveness Is an Act of Love

The story for this lesson is an adaptation of Matthew 18:21–35. It is important that the children understand that we all make wrong choices, sometimes causing hurt or unhappiness to others. This does not mean that we are bad persons, but rather that the deed is wrong and unacceptable to God. When we have done wrong, it does not mean that God and the person we have offended no longer love us, but rather that we have hurt them and need to ask for forgiveness. Saying "I'm sorry" is only half of asking for forgiveness. We must also show through our actions that we are truly sorry and will try to do better.

Concepts of Faith

Whom do we ask to forgive us when we do something wrong?
When we do something wrong, we ask God and the person we have hurt or disobeyed to forgive us.

How should we forgive others?
We should forgive others as God forgives us.

Correspondence to the *Catechism of the Catholic Church*

The Sacrament of Penance and Reconciliation: *CCC* 1440–45, 1487
The acts of the penitent: *CCC* 1450–53
Satisfaction: *CCC* 1459

Suggested Activity

Help your child say "I'm sorry" and ask forgiveness from someone who has been offended.

Our Father Booklet

Our Father, who art in heaven,

God, our Father, is in heaven.

hallowed be thy name.

GOD

God's name is holy.

Family Note

Lesson 10: Prayer

The story for this lesson is an adaptation of Luke 18:9–14. The Our Father is introduced in this lesson. Jesus prayed often and taught others how to pray. Jesus wants us to follow his example and pray often to our Father in heaven. God hears all our prayers even when we do not say the words out loud. Sometimes we do not get what we pray for because God knows what is best for us.

Concepts of Faith

What is prayer?

Prayer is raising our hearts and minds to God by talking with him. We can pray quietly or out loud, alone or with others. We can say "thank you", ask for help, say "I'm sorry", adore God, and sing God's praises.

Correspondence to the *Catechism of the Catholic Church*

Prayer as God's gift: *CCC* 2559–65, 2590, 2644
In the fullness of time: *CCC* 2598–606, 2620
Jesus teaches how to pray: *CCC* 2607–15, 2621
Jesus hears our prayers: *CCC* 2616, 2621
Blessing and adoration: *CCC* 2626–28, 2645
Prayer of petition: *CCC* 2629–33, 2646
Prayers of intercession: *CCC* 2634–36, 2647
Prayer of thanksgiving: *CCC* 2637–38, 2648
Prayers of praise: *CCC* 2639–43, 2649
Prayer to the Father: *CCC* 2664, 2680
Prayer to Jesus: *CCC* 2665–69, 2680
"Come, Holy Spirit": *CCC* 2670–72, 2681
In communion with the holy Mother of God: *CCC* 2673–79, 2682
A cloud of witnesses: *CCC* 2683–84, 2692
Places favorable for prayer: *CCC* 2691, 2696
Filial trust: *CCC* 2734–41, 2756
"The summary of the whole gospel": *CCC* 2761–76
The seven petitions: *CCC* 2803–6, 2857
"We Dare to Say": *CCC* 2777–96, 2797–802
"Hallowed Be Thy Name": *CCC* 2807–15, 2858
"Thy Kingdom Come": *CCC* 2816–21, 2859
"The Will Be Done on Earth as It Is in Heaven": *CCC* 2822–27, 2860
"Give Us This Day Our Daily Bread": *CCC* 2828–37, 2861
"Forgive Us Our Trespasses, as We Forgive Those Who Trespass Against Us": *CCC* 2838–45, 2862
"And Lead Us Not into Temptation": *CCC* 2846–49, 2863
"But Deliver Us from Evil": *CCC* 2850–54, 2864
The final doxology: *CCC* 2855–56, 2865

Suggested Activity

Review the Our Father with your child.

Our Father Booklet

Thy kingdom come. Thy will be done on earth, as it is in heaven.

We will try to live as images of God on earth.

Give us this day our daily bread,

Give us what we need to live now and later with you in heaven.

and forgive us our trespasses, as we forgive those who trespass against us,

Forgive us for our sins and help us forgive others.

**and lead us not into temptation,
but deliver us from evil. Amen.**

*Help us to make good choices
and keep us safe in your love.*

Our Father Booklet

Directions: Connect the dots and color the picture.

The woman found something much better than water.

Family Note

Lesson 11: Jesus Is God the Son

The story for this lesson is an adaptation of John 4:4–30. Jesus is God the Son, the second person of the Blessed Trinity. Jesus is the one whose coming was foretold in the Scriptures. He came down from heaven to save us from our sins—that is, to redeem us. Thus, he shows us who we are and makes it possible for us to live as images of God now and to be happy forever with God in heaven.

Concepts of Faith

Who is Jesus?

Jesus is God the Son, the second person of the Blessed Trinity.

Correspondence to the *Catechism of the Catholic Church*

Jesus: *CCC* 430–35
The only Son of God: *CCC* 441–45, 454
The Son of God became man: *CCC* 456–63

Suggested Activity

Show your child your family Bible or a Bible you use.

Directions: Color the dotted areas.

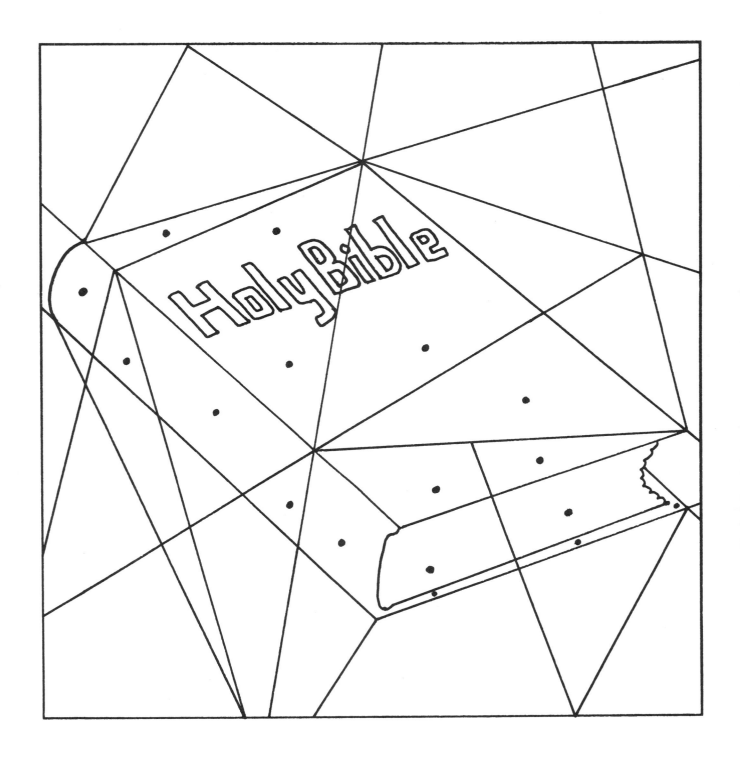

The Bible is a book about God and Jesus' life on earth.

Family Note

Lesson 11: Jesus Is God the Son

The story for this lesson is an adaptation of John 4:4–30. Jesus is God the Son, the second person of the Blessed Trinity. Jesus is the one whose coming was foretold in the Scriptures. He came down from heaven to save us from our sins—that is, to redeem us. Thus, he shows us who we are and makes it possible for us to live as images of God now and to be happy forever with God in heaven.

Concepts of Faith

Who is Jesus?

Jesus is God the Son, the second person of the Blessed Trinity.

Correspondence to the *Catechism of the Catholic Church*

Jesus: *CCC* 430–35
The only Son of God: *CCC* 441–45, 454
The Son of God became man: *CCC* 456–63

Suggested Activity

Show your child your family Bible or a Bible you use.

Directions: Connect the dots and color the picture.

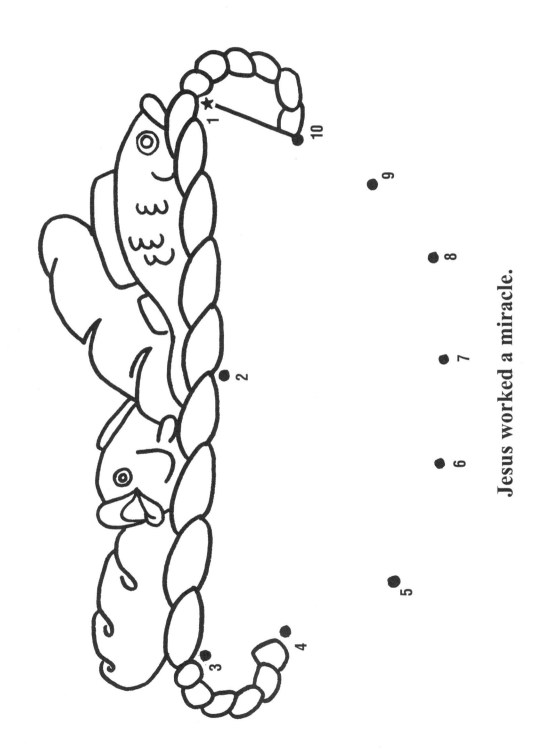

Jesus worked a miracle.

Family Note

Lesson 12: Miracles of Jesus

The story for this lesson is an adaptation of John 6:1–15. The miracles that Jesus performed were not magic tricks. Jesus really did heal the sick, change water into wine, and multiply the loaves and fishes. He could perform miracles because he is God the Son. The miracles Jesus worked helped people believe in what he said. As images of God, we can help others believe in and follow Jesus.

Concepts of Faith

Who is Jesus?

Jesus is God the Son, the second person of the Blessed Trinity, made man.

Correspondence to the *Catechism of the Catholic Church*

The signs of the kingdom of God: *CCC 547–50*

Suggested Activity

Work together with your child to do something nice for another member of your family. Talk about how Jesus helped others.

Directions: Circle the miracles.

Jesus can work miracles because he is God the Son.

Family Note

Lesson 12: Miracles of Jesus

The story for this lesson is an adaptation of John 6:1–15. The miracles that Jesus performed were not magic tricks. Jesus really did heal the sick, change water into wine, and multiply the loaves and fishes. He could perform miracles because he is God the Son. The miracles Jesus worked helped people believe in what he said. As images of God, we can help others believe in and follow Jesus.

Concepts of Faith

Who is Jesus?

Jesus is God the Son, the second person of the Blessed Trinity, made man.

Correspondence to the *Catechism of the Catholic Church*

The signs of the kingdom of God: *CCC* 547–50

Suggested Activity

Work together with your child to do something nice for another member of your family. Talk about how Jesus helped others.

Directions: Find and color the hidden fish.

Jesus asked the fishermen to follow him.

Family Note

Lesson 13: Jesus Says, "Come Follow Me"

The story for this lesson is an adaptation of Matthew 4:18–22. Jesus extended the invitation to follow him repeatedly throughout his life on earth. He extended a special invitation to follow him and to do as he did to the Apostles. They answered Jesus' call and chose to follow him and to lead others to him. Jesus asks all people to follow him. We follow Jesus by being the best images of God we can be.

Concepts of Faith

Who were the Apostles?

The Apostles were special friends of Jesus' who answered his call and chose to follow him. They answered Jesus' call and were sent by him to teach others about him and to do his work in a special way.

Correspondence to the *Catechism of the Catholic Church*

The Church is apostolic: *CCC* 857
The Apostles' mission: *CCC* 858–60
The bishops—successors of the Apostles: *CCC* 861–62

Suggested Activity

Play "follow the leader" with your child.

Directions: Follow the footprints to heaven.

Jesus said, "Come follow me."

Family Note

Lesson 13: Jesus Says, "Come Follow Me"

The story for this lesson is an adaptation of Matthew 4:18–22. Jesus extended the invitation to follow him repeatedly throughout his life on earth. He extended a special invitation to follow him and to do as he did to the Apostles. They answered Jesus' call and chose to follow him and to lead others to him. Jesus asks all people to follow him. We follow Jesus by being the best images of God we can be.

Concepts of Faith

Who were the Apostles?

The Apostles were special friends of Jesus' who answered his call and chose to follow him. They answered Jesus' call and were sent by him to teach others about him and to do his work in a special way.

Correspondence to the *Catechism of the Catholic Church*

The Church is apostolic: *CCC* 857
The Apostles' mission: *CCC* 858–60
The bishops—successors of the Apostles: *CCC* 861–62

Suggested Activity

Play "follow the leader" with your child.

Directions: Connect the dots and color the picture.

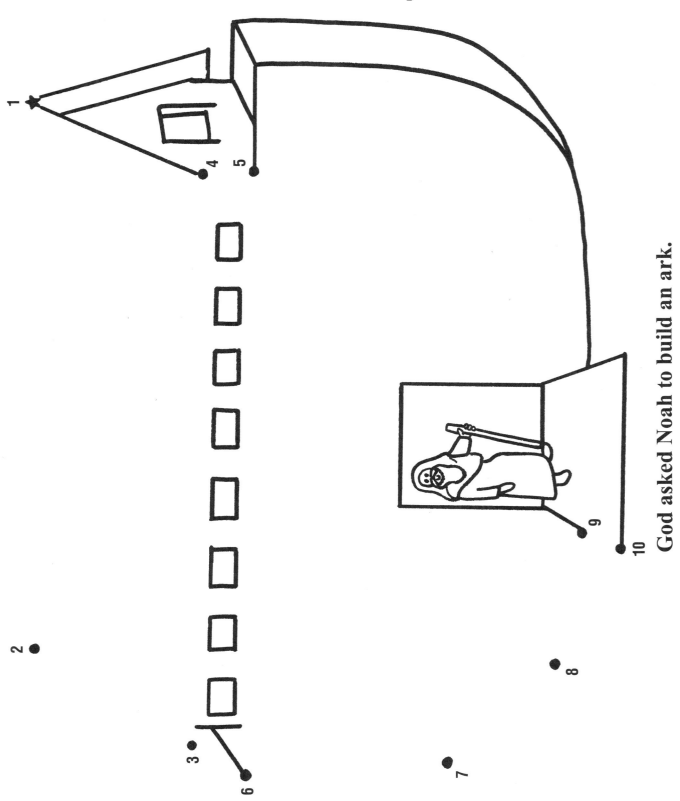

God asked Noah to build an ark.

Family Note

Lesson 14: Faith and Trust

The story for this lesson is an adaptation of Genesis 6:14–22, 8:6–12, and 9:8–17. God made us to do good things. When we live good lives, we are showing our faith and saying "Yes" to God. Jesus, God the Son, teaches us what are truly good actions. By following Jesus' example and the teachings of his Church, we practice our faith and show God our love.

Concepts of Faith

What is faith?

Faith is the power that God gives us that helps us believe in him and all he has taught.

Correspondence to the *Catechism of the Catholic Church*

Faith: *CCC* 26, 142, 150, 153, 1814, 2087
Trust: *CCC* 301, 304, 2115, 2547, 2828, 2836, 2861

Suggested Activity

Read a Bible story to your child.

Directions: Connect the matching animals.

Noah led two of every animal to the ark.

Family Note

Lesson 14: Faith and Trust

The story for this lesson is an adaptation of Genesis 6:14–22, 8:6–12, and 9:8–17. God made us to do good things. When we live good lives, we are showing our faith and saying "Yes" to God. Jesus, God the Son, teaches us what are truly good actions. By following Jesus' example and the teachings of his Church, we practice our faith and show God our love.

Concepts of Faith

What is faith?
Faith is the power that God gives us that helps us believe in him and all he has taught.

Correspondence to the *Catechism of the Catholic Church*

Faith: *CCC* 26, 142, 150, 153, 1814, 2087
Trust: *CCC* 301, 304, 2115, 2547, 2828, 2836, 2861

Suggested Activity

Read a Bible story to your child.

Directions: Color the picture.

Jesus said, "Little girl, get up."

Family Note

Lesson 15: After Death There Is Life

The story for this lesson is an adaptation of Mark 5:21–24 and 5:35–43. When someone dies, that person's life does not end; it changes. When people die, they begin new lives with God in heaven, if they have followed Jesus' example. We are still images of God even after we have died. We pray for all those who have died so they may receive new life with God in heaven.

Concepts of Faith

Is dying the end of our lives?
No. If we have lived as images of God, it is the beginning of new life with God in heaven.

Correspondence to the *Catechism of the Catholic Church*

"I believe in the resurrection of the body": *CCC* 988–91, 1015–19
Christ's Resurrection and ours: *CCC* 992–1004
Dying in Christ Jesus: *CCC* 1005–14

Suggested Activity

Tell your child about a relative or friend who has died. Say a prayer with your child for that person.

Directions: Cut out the wings. Put them on the butterfly.

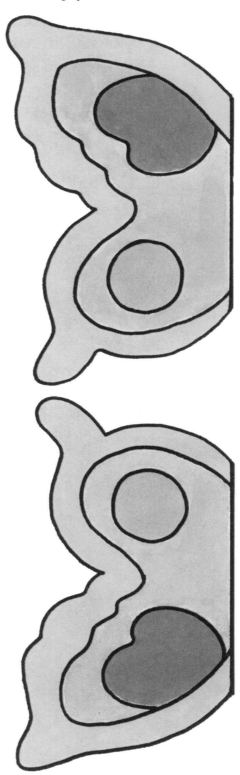

A butterfly is a sign of new life.

Family Note

Lesson 15: After Death There Is Life

The story for this lesson is an adaptation of Mark 5:21–24 and 5:35–43. When someone dies, that person's life does not end; it changes. When people die, they begin new lives with God in heaven, if they have followed Jesus' example. We are still images of God even after we have died. We pray for all those who have died so they may receive new life with God in heaven.

Concepts of Faith

Is dying the end of our lives?
No. If we have lived as images of God, it is the beginning of new life with God in heaven.

Correspondence to the *Catechism of the Catholic Church*

"I believe in the resurrection of the body": *CCC* 988–91, 1015–19
Christ's Resurrection and ours: *CCC* 992–1004
Dying in Christ Jesus: *CCC* 1005–14

Suggested Activity

Tell your child about a relative or friend who has died. Say a prayer with your child for that person.

Directions: Circle the good actions.

**Our good actions show that God
is most important in our lives.**

Family Note

Lesson 16: God Should Come First in Our Lives

The story for this lesson is an adaptation of Matthew 7:24–29. When we live our lives showing that we are images of God in all we think, and say, and do, then we show that God comes first for us. It may not always be easy to do what is right, but when we obey and think of others before ourselves, we are living as Jesus taught and showing that God is most important in our lives. The material things we have—toys, jewelry, houses, money, etc.—are good and are for our use, but they are not the most important part of life. God should be first in our lives.

Concepts of Faith

Who is most important in our lives?
God is most important in our lives.

How do we show that God is most important?
We show that God is most important by acting as images of God in all we think, say, and do.

Correspondence to the *Catechism of the Catholic Church*

Heaven: *CCC* 1023–29, 1052–53
Jesus teaches how to pray: *CCC* 2607–15, 2621
New law or law of the Gospel: *CCC* 1965–74, 1977, 1983–86
What is prayer?: *CCC* 2559–65, 2590, 2644

Suggested Activity

Have your child gather some outgrown toys or clothes to give to the needy.

Directions: Color the picture.

**The wise man built his house on the rock.
We should build our lives with God.**

Family Note

Lesson 16: God Should Come First in Our Lives

The story for this lesson is an adaptation of Matthew 7:24–29. When we live our lives showing that we are images of God in all we think, and say, and do, then we show that God comes first for us. It may not always be easy to do what is right, but when we obey and think of others before ourselves, we are living as Jesus taught and showing that God is most important in our lives. The material things we have—toys, jewelry, houses, money, etc.—are good and are for our use, but they are not the most important part of life. God should be first in our lives.

Concepts of Faith

Who is most important in our lives?
God is most important in our lives.

How do we show that God is most important?
We show that God is most important by acting as images of God in all we think, say, and do.

Correspondence to the *Catechism of the Catholic Church*

Heaven: *CCC* 1023–29, 1052–53
Jesus teaches how to pray: *CCC* 2607–15, 2621
New law or law of the Gospel: *CCC* 1965–74, 1977, 1983–86
What is prayer?: *CCC* 2559–65, 2590, 2644

Suggested Activity

Have your child gather some outgrown toys or clothes to give to the needy.

Directions: Help the shepherd find his lost sheep.

The good shepherd took care of his sheep.

Family Note

Lesson 17: God Cares for Us and All He Has Made

The story for this lesson is an adaptation of Matthew 18:10–14 and John 10:1–15. God is the source of all we have and all we need. He loves us. He wants to share his life with us now and he wants us to be with him someday in heaven. God has told us, shown us, and given us all that we need to be the best images of God we can be. Jesus told us that God takes care of all that he has made. We know God loves and takes care of us.

Concepts of Faith

Who takes care of us always?
God takes care of us always.

Whom did God give to each one of us to help and guide us?
God gave each one of us a guardian angel to help and guide us.

Correspondence to the *Catechism of the Catholic Church*

The existence of angels—a truth of faith: *CCC 328*
Who are they?: *CCC 329–30, 350*
Christ "with all his angels": *CCC 331–33, 351*
The angels in the life of the Church: *CCC 334–36, 352*

Suggested Activity

Review the Guardian Angel Prayer with your child:

> *Angel of God,*
> *my guardian dear,*
> *to whom God's love commits me here,*
> *ever this day be at my side,*
> *to light and guard, to rule and guide.*
> *Amen.*

Directions: Color the dotted areas.

**Jesus is our Good Shepherd.
He loves and takes care of us.**

Family Note

Lesson 17: God Cares for Us and All He Has Made

The story for this lesson is an adaptation of Matthew 18:10–14 and John 10:1–15. God is the source of all we have and all we need. He loves us. He wants to share his life with us now and he wants us to be with him someday in heaven. God has told us, shown us, and given us all that we need to be the best images of God we can be. Jesus told us that God takes care of all that he has made. We know God loves and takes care of us.

Concepts of Faith

Who takes care of us always?
God takes care of us always.

Whom did God give to each one of us to help and guide us?
God gave each one of us a guardian angel to help and guide us.

Correspondence to the *Catechism of the Catholic Church*

The existence of angels—a truth of faith: *CCC* 328
Who are they?: *CCC* 329–30, 350
Christ "with all his angels": *CCC* 331–33, 351
The angels in the life of the Church: *CCC* 334–36, 352

Suggested Activity

Review the Guardian Angel Prayer with your child:

Angel of God,
my guardian dear,
to whom God's love commits me here,
ever this day be at my side,
to light and guard, to rule and guide.
Amen.

Directions: Cut out the food. Put the food on the plate.

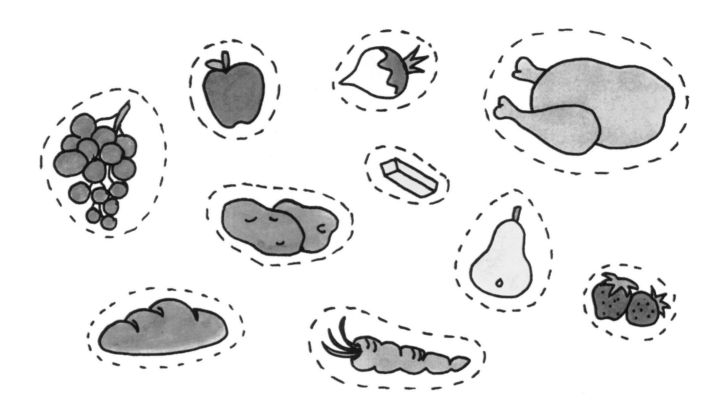

Thank you, God, for all you have given us.

Family Note

Lesson 18: Thanksgiving

The story for this lesson is an adaptation of Luke 17:11–19. Thanksgiving is not just a time for a big meal with family and friends. It is a time for all of God's family to join together to say "thank you" and to give praise to our loving Father who made all things. Through our prayers, we thank God for all he has given us. We also show God we are thankful by taking care of what he has given us.

Correspondence to the *Catechism of the Catholic Church*

Liturgical celebration: *CCC* 1145–62, 1189–92
Liturgical seasons: *CCC* 1163–65
Liturgical year: *CCC* 1168–71, 1194
Prayers of thanksgiving: *CCC* 2637–38, 2648

Suggested Activity

Recite the Blessing before Meals with your child:

Bless us, O Lord, and these thy gifts
which we are about to receive from thy bounty,
through Christ, our Lord. Amen.

Directions: Circle the items that remind us of Jesus' birthday

During Advent, we prepare our hearts and homes for Jesus' birthday.

Family Note

Lesson 19: First Week of Advent—Preparing Our Hearts and Homes

As we wait for the celebration of Jesus' birthday, Christmas, we prepare our homes, and more importantly, our hearts. During the waiting period, Advent, there are many ways in which we can show our love for God and others. It is important we share the true meaning of Christmas—that is, love—in our daily lives throughout the entire year and not just during this season.

Concepts of Faith

Who is Jesus?
Jesus is God the Son.

When do we celebrate Jesus' birthday?
We celebrate Jesus' birthday on Christmas.

Correspondence to the *Catechism of the Catholic Church*

Preparations for Christ's coming: *CCC 522–24*
Advent: *CCC 524, 1095*
Christmas mystery: *CCC 525–26, 563*
Mysteries of Jesus' infancy: *CCC 527–30*
Liturgical seasons: *CCC 1163–65*
Liturgical year: *CCC 1168–71, 1194*

Suggested Activity

Use an Advent wreath with your family to count the weeks until Christmas.

Directions: Cut out the candles. Glue them on the wreath.

Advent is a time of waiting for Jesus' birthday.

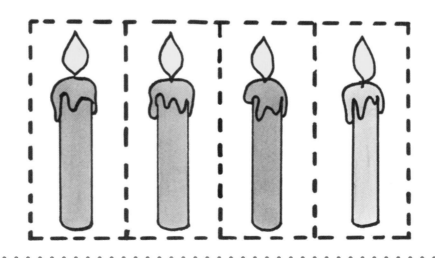

Family Note

Lesson 19: First Week of Advent—Preparing Our Hearts and Homes

As we wait for the celebration of Jesus' birthday, Christmas, we prepare our homes, and more importantly, our hearts. During the waiting period, Advent, there are many ways in which we can show our love for God and others. It is important we share the true meaning of Christmas—that is, love—in our daily lives throughout the entire year and not just during this season.

Concepts of Faith

Who is Jesus?
Jesus is God the Son.

When do we celebrate Jesus' birthday?
We celebrate Jesus' birthday on Christmas.

Correspondence to the *Catechism of the Catholic Church*

Preparations for Christ's coming: *CCC* 522–24
Advent: *CCC* 524, 1095
Christmas mystery: *CCC* 525–26, 563
Mysteries of Jesus' infancy: *CCC* 527–30
Liturgical seasons: *CCC* 1163–65
Liturgical year: *CCC* 1168–71, 1194

Suggested Activity

Use an Advent wreath with your family to count the weeks until Christmas.

Directions: Cut out baby Jesus. Lay him in Mary's arms.

Mary is Jesus' mother.

Family Note

Lesson 20: Second Week of Advent—Mary Said "Yes" to God

The story for this lesson is an adaptation of Luke 1:26–45. Mary willingly chose to do what God asked her to do. Mary is an example for all people. She showed her love for God in all she thought, said, and did. We should follow her example. We ask Mary to pray for all of us so we will be more like her and her Son, Jesus.

Concepts of Faith

Who is Mary?
Mary is the Mother of God.

Correspondence to the *Catechism of the Catholic Church*

Conceived by the power of the Holy Spirit: *CCC* 484–86
Born of the Virgin Mary: *CCC* 487
Mary's predestination: *CCC* 488–89
The Immaculate Conception: *CCC* 490–93, 508
"Let it be done to me according to your word…": *CCC* 494
Mary's divine motherhood: *CCC* 495, 509
Mary's virginity: *CCC* 496–98
Mary—"ever-virgin": *CCC* 499–501, 510
Mary's virginal motherhood in God's plan: *CCC* 502–7, 511
Preparations for Christ's coming: *CCC* 522–24
Advent: *CCC* 524, 1095
Christmas mystery: *CCC* 525–26, 563
Mysteries of Jesus' infancy: *CCC* 527–30
"Rejoice, you who are full of grace": *CCC* 721–26, 744
Mary—Mother of Christ, Mother of the Church: *CCC* 963
Wholly united with her Son: *CCC* 964–65
"… also in her Assumption": *CCC* 966, 973–75
"… she is our Mother in the order of grace": *CCC* 967–70
Devotion to the Blessed Virgin: *CCC* 971
Mary—Eschatological icon of the Church: *CCC* 972
The sanctoral in the liturgical year: *CCC* 1172
In communion with the holy Mother of God: *CCC* 2676–77

Suggested Activity

Recite the Hail Mary with your child:

Hail Mary, full of grace, the Lord is with thee.
Blessed art thou among women, and blessed is the fruit of thy womb, Jesus.
Holy Mary, Mother of God, pray for us sinners, now and at the hour of our death.
Amen.

Directions: Circle the things Mary would need for baby Jesus.

Mary loves and cares for Jesus like our mothers take care of us.

Family Note

Lesson 20: Second Week of Advent—Mary Said "Yes" to God

The story for this lesson is an adaptation of Luke 1:26–45. Mary willingly chose to do what God asked her to do. Mary is an example for all people. She showed her love for God in all she thought, said, and did. We should follow her example. We ask Mary to pray for all of us so we will be more like her and her Son, Jesus.

Concepts of Faith

Who is Mary?
Mary is the Mother of God.

Correspondence to the *Catechism of the Catholic Church*

Conceived by the power of the Holy Spirit: *CCC* 484–86
Born of the Virgin Mary: *CCC* 487
Mary's predestination: *CCC* 488–89
The Immaculate Conception: *CCC* 490–93, 508
"Let it be done to me according to your word…": *CCC* 494
Mary's divine motherhood: *CCC* 495, 509
Mary's virginity: *CCC* 496–98
Mary—"ever-virgin": *CCC* 499–501, 510
Mary's virginal motherhood in God's plan: *CCC* 502–7, 511
Preparations for Christ's coming: *CCC* 522–24
Advent: *CCC* 524, 1095
Christmas mystery: *CCC* 525–26, 563
Mysteries of Jesus' infancy: *CCC* 527–30
"Rejoice, you who are full of grace": *CCC* 721–26, 744
Mary—Mother of Christ, Mother of the Church: *CCC* 963
Wholly united with her Son: *CCC* 964–65
"… also in her Assumption": *CCC* 966, 973–75
"… she is our Mother in the order of grace": *CCC* 967–70
Devotion to the Blessed Virgin: *CCC* 971
Mary—Eschatological icon of the Church: *CCC* 972
The sanctoral in the liturgical year: *CCC* 1172
In communion with the holy Mother of God: *CCC* 2676–77

Suggested Activity

Recite the Hail Mary with your child:

Hail Mary, full of grace, the Lord is with thee.
Blessed art thou among women, and blessed is the fruit of thy womb, Jesus.
Holy Mary, Mother of God, pray for us sinners, now and at the hour of our death.
Amen.

Directions: Connect the dots and color the picture.

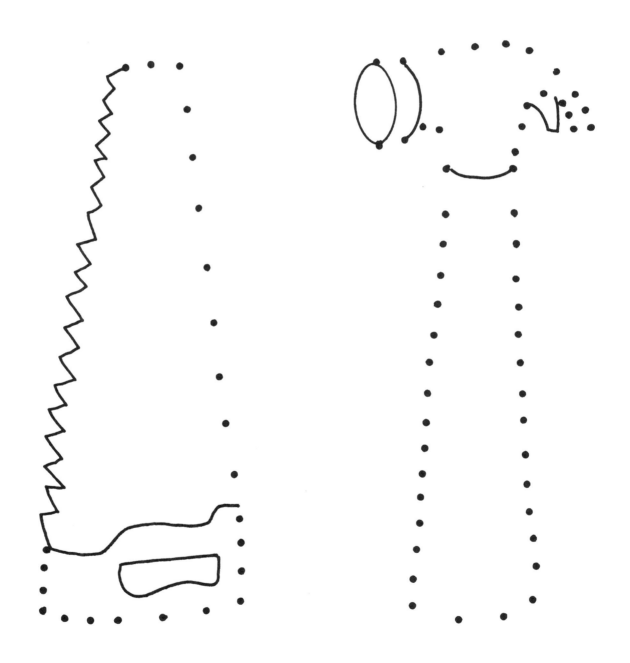

Joseph was a carpenter.
He made things out of wood.

Family Note

Lesson 21: Third Week of Advent—Joseph, Jesus' Father on Earth

The story for this lesson is an adaptation of Matthew 1:18–25 and Luke 2:1–7. Joseph received special graces from God to be the head of the Holy Family. He was chosen by God to be Jesus' foster father and Mary's husband. Like Jesus and Mary, Joseph chose to obey the will of God in all things. He cared for Jesus and Mary out of love for them and for God.

Concepts of Faith

Who was Joseph?
Joseph was Jesus' father on earth.

Correspondence to the *Catechism of the Catholic Church*

Annunciation of the angel to Joseph: *CCC* 497, 1846
Feast day of Saint Joseph: *CCC* 2177
Jesus' submission to Joseph: *CCC* 532
Mysteries of Jesus' infancy: *CCC* 527–30
Patron of a happy death: *CCC* 1014
Role and calling of Joseph: *CCC* 437

Suggested Activity

Help your child make a Christmas present for someone as a gift of love.

Directions: Help Joseph and Mary find the stable.

Joseph and Mary traveled to Bethlehem.

Family Note

Lesson 21: Third Week of Advent—Joseph, Jesus' Father on Earth

The story for this lesson is an adaptation of Matthew 1:18–25 and Luke 2:1–7. Joseph received special graces from God to be the head of the Holy Family. He was chosen by God to be Jesus' foster father and Mary's husband. Like Jesus and Mary, Joseph chose to obey the will of God in all things. He cared for Jesus and Mary out of love for them and for God.

Concepts of Faith

Who was Joseph?
Joseph was Jesus' father on earth.

Correspondence to the *Catechism of the Catholic Church*

Annunciation of the angel to Joseph: *CCC* 497, 1846
Feast day of Saint Joseph: *CCC* 2177
Jesus' submission to Joseph: *CCC* 532
Mysteries of Jesus' infancy: *CCC* 527–30
Patron of a happy death: *CCC* 1014
Role and calling of Joseph: *CCC* 437

Suggested Activity

Help your child make a Christmas present for someone as a gift of love.

Directions: Connect the dots and color the picture.

Jesus' bed was called a manger.

Family Note

Lesson 22: Fourth Week of Advent—Christmas Is Jesus' Birthday

The story for this lesson is an adaptation of Luke 2:1–18. Jesus teaches us that life is truly a celebration of love to be offered to God. On his birthday, we renew our commitment to a life of love and pray that our hearts be filled with the peace and love of the Christ child. Christmas is a worldwide celebration of love—the love God has for us and the love we have for God and others.

Concepts of Faith

What is Christmas?

Christmas is the feast day of the birth of Jesus.

Correspondence to the *Catechism of the Catholic Church*

Announcement to the shepherds: *CCC* 437
Christmas mystery: *CCC* 525–26, 563
Mysteries of Jesus' infancy: *CCC* 527–30

Suggested Activity

Help your child set up a Nativity scene in anticipation of Christmas.

Directions: Cut out the figure of baby Jesus. Lay him in the manger.

Mary laid baby Jesus in the manger.

Family Note

Lesson 22: Fourth Week of Advent—Christmas Is Jesus' Birthday

The story for this lesson is an adaptation of Luke 2:1–18. Jesus teaches us that life is truly a celebration of love to be offered to God. On His birthday, we renew our commitment to a life of love and pray that our hearts be filled with the peace and love of the Christ child. Christmas is a worldwide celebration of love—the love God has for us and the love we have for God and others.

Concepts of Faith

What is Christmas?
Christmas is the feast day of the birth of Jesus.

Correspondence to the *Catechism of the Catholic Church*

Announcement to the shepherds: *CCC* 437
Christmas mystery: *CCC* 525–26, 563
Mysteries of Jesus' infancy: *CCC* 527–30

Suggested Activity

Help your child set up a Nativity scene in anticipation of Christmas.

Directions: Circle the things that remind us Easter is near.

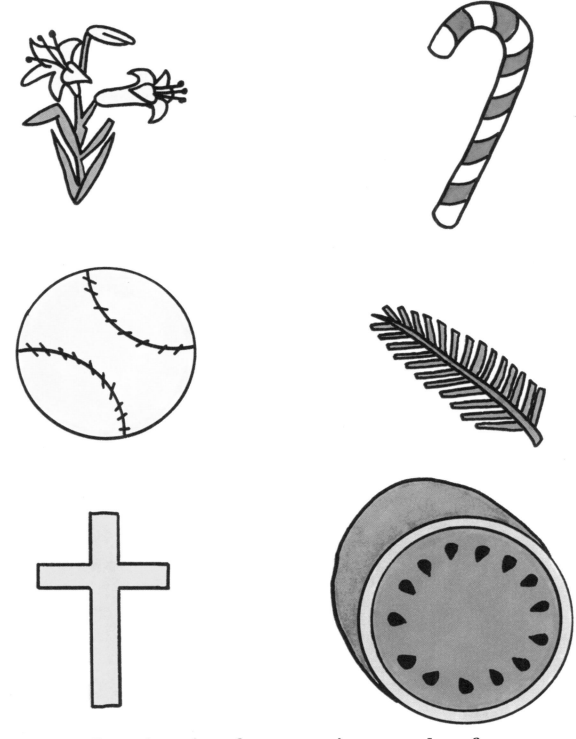

**Lent is a time for preparing ourselves for
the joy and new life of Easter.**

Family Note

Lesson 23: Lent

During Lent, we make sacrifices to offer to God. We choose to do without things such as a favorite television show or treats. We give up something to show God we love him, and that he is most important to us. Jesus gave up his life for us because he loves us.

Concepts of Faith

What is Lent?

Lent is a time for preparing ourselves for the joy and new life (grace) of Easter.

Correspondence to the *Catechism of the Catholic Church*

Forms of penance in Christian life: *CCC* 1434–39
Sacrifice: *CCC* 2099–100
Lent: *CCC* 540, 1095, 1438
Jesus as our teacher and model of holiness: *CCC* 516, 519–21, 561
Christ's whole life as a self-offering to the Father: *CCC* 606–18, 621–23
Christ's redemptive Death in the divine plan of salvation: *CCC* 599–605, 619–20
Prayer to Jesus: *CCC* 2669

Suggested Activity

As a family, decide to do something during Lent that shows God you love him.

Directions: Connect the dots and color the picture.

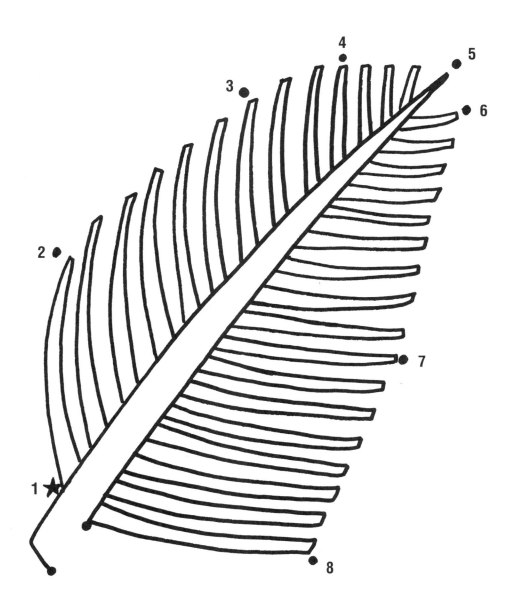

**The people shouted "Hosanna" and laid
palm branches on the road.**

Family Note

Lesson 24: Palm Sunday

Palm Sunday is the beginning of Holy Week. On the first Palm Sunday, Jesus entered Jerusalem amid the cheers and the praises of the people, in sharp contrast to what would happen to him at the end of Holy Week.

Concepts of Faith

What happened on Palm Sunday?

Jesus entered Jerusalem amid shouts of praise.

Correspondence to the *Catechism of the Catholic Church*

Christ's redemptive Death in the divine plan of salvation: *CCC* 599–605, 619–20
Christ's whole life as a self-offering to the Father: *CCC* 606–18, 621–23
Jesus freely embraces the Father's redemptive love: *CCC* 609

Suggested Activity

Show your child the palm branches given out at church. Tell your child the story of Jesus' triumphant entrance into Jerusalem.

Directions: Trace the letters.

THIS IS MY
BODY

Family Note

Lesson 25: Holy Week

Holy Week includes Palm Sunday, the day people sang "Hosanna" to Jesus; Holy Thursday, the day of the Last Supper; Good Friday, the day Jesus died; and Holy Saturday, the day Jesus' body lay in the tomb.

Concepts of Faith

What happened on Holy Thursday?
On Holy Thursday, Jesus and the Apostles shared the Last Supper, the first Mass.

What happened on Good Friday?
On Good Friday, Jesus died on the Cross.

Correspondence to the *Catechism of the Catholic Church*

Death of Christ as the unique and definitive sacrifice: *CCC* 613–14
Jesus substitutes his obedience for our disobedience: *CCC* 615
Jesus consummates his sacrifice on the cross: *CCC* 616–17
Our participation in Christ's sacrifice: *CCC* 618

Suggested Activity

Show your child a picture of the Last Supper and a picture of Jesus on the Cross.

Directions: Connect the dots and color the picture.

Alleluia! He is risen.

Family Note

Lesson 26: Easter Sunday

Easter is the celebration of new life. At this time, we remember Jesus' triumph over Death, his Resurrection. Easter is the most joyous feast of the Church, celebrating the new life we receive from Jesus. We want to live with Jesus now, and someday we hope to be with him in heaven.

Concepts of Faith

What happened on Easter Sunday?

On Easter Sunday, Jesus rose from the dead.

Correspondence to the *Catechism of the Catholic Church*

The liturgical year: *CCC* 1168–70

Suggested Activity

Go on a spring walk with your child. Look for signs of new life.

Directions: Color the dotted areas.

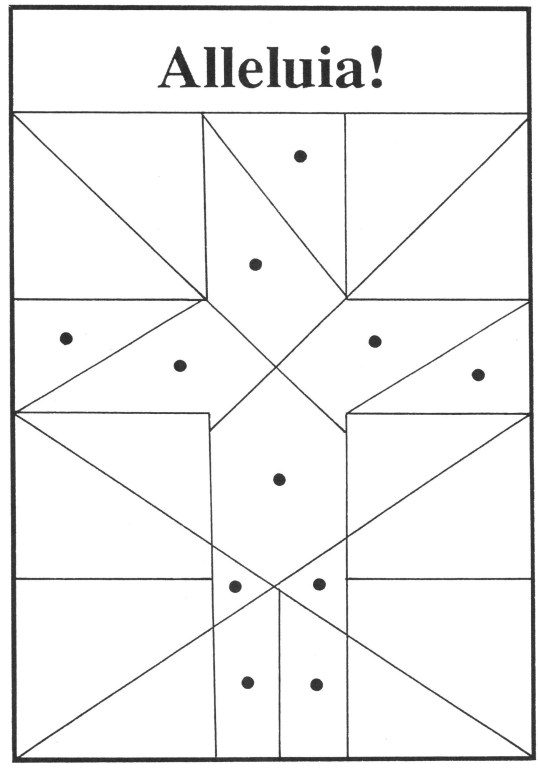

Alleluia! He is risen.

Family Note

Lesson 26: Easter Sunday

Easter is the celebration of new life. At this time, we remember Jesus' triumph over Death, his Resurrection. Easter is the most joyous feast of the Church, celebrating the new life we receive from Jesus. We want to live with Jesus now, and someday we hope to be with him in heaven.

Concepts of Faith

What happened on Easter Sunday?

On Easter Sunday, Jesus rose from the dead.

Correspondence to the *Catechism of the Catholic Church*

The liturgical year: *CCC* 1168–70

Suggested Activity

Go on a spring walk with your child. Look for signs of new life.

Our Father

Our Father who art in heaven,
hallowed be thy name.
Thy kingdom come.
Thy will be done on earth, as it is in heaven.
Give us this day our daily bread,
and forgive us our trespasses, as we forgive those who trespass against us,
and lead us not into temptation, but deliver us from evil.
Amen.

Apostles' Creed

I believe in God, the Father almighty,
Creator of heaven and earth,
and in Jesus Christ, his only Son, our Lord,
who was conceived by the Holy Spirit,
born of the Virgin Mary,
suffered under Pontius Pilate,
was crucified, died, and was buried;
he descended into hell;
on the third day he rose again from the dead;
he ascended into heaven,
and is seated at the right hand of God the Father almighty;
from there he will come to judge the living and the dead.
I believe in the Holy Spirit,
the holy catholic Church,
the communion of saints,
the forgiveness of sins,
the resurrection of the body,
and life everlasting.
Amen.

Glory Be

Glory be to the Father and to the Son and to the Holy Spirit,
as it was in the beginning is now, and ever shall be world without end.
Amen.

Hail Mary

Hail, Mary, full of grace, the Lord is with thee.
Blessed art thou among women and blessed is the fruit of thy womb, Jesus.
Holy Mary, Mother of God, pray for us sinners now, and at the hour of our death.
Amen.

Hail, Holy Queen

Hail, Holy Queen, Mother of Mercy,
our life, our sweetness and our hope.
To thee do we cry, poor banished children of Eve.
To thee do we send up our sighs,
mourning and weeping in this valley of tears.
Turn then, most gracious advocate,
thine eyes of mercy toward us,
and after this exile,
show unto us the blessed fruit of thy womb, Jesus.
O clement, O loving, O sweet Virgin Mary.
   V. Pray for us, O holy Mother of God.
   R. That we may be made worthy of the promises of Christ.

Memorare

Remember, O most gracious Virgin Mary,
that never was it known
that anyone who fled to thy protection,
implored thy help,
or sought thy intercession,
was left unaided.
Inspired by this confidence
I fly unto thee, O Virgin of virgins, my Mother.
To thee do I come, before thee I stand, sinful and sorrowful.
O Mother of the Word Incarnate.
despise not my petitions,
but in thy mercy hear and answer me.
Amen.

Angelus

The Angel of the Lord declared unto Mary.
And she conceived of the Holy Spirit.

Hail, Mary, . . .

Behold the handmaid of the Lord.
Be it done unto me according to thy word.

Hail, Mary, . . .

And the Word was made flesh.
And dwelt among us.

Hail, Mary, . . .

Pray for us, O holy Mother of God.
That we may be made worthy of the promises of Christ.
Let us pray:

Pour forth, we beseech thee, O Lord, thy grace into our hearts; that we,
to whom the Incarnation of Christ, thy Son, was made known by the message
of an angel, may by his Passion and Cross be brought to the glory of his
Resurrection, through the same Christ, our Lord. Amen.

Act of Contrition

My God,
I am sorry for my sins with all my heart.
In choosing to do wrong and failing to do good,
I have sinned against you
whom I should love above all things.
I firmly intend, with your help,
to do penance, to sin no more,
and to avoid whatever leads me to sin.
Our Savior Jesus Christ suffered and died for us.
In his name, my God, have mercy.
Amen.

An Act of Faith

O my God, I firmly believe that you are one God in three divine persons,
Father, Son, and Holy Spirit.
I believe that your divine Son became man and died for our sins
and that he will come to judge the living and the dead.
I believe these and all the truths which the Holy Catholic Church teaches
because you have revealed them who are eternal truth and wisdom,
who can neither deceive nor be deceived.
In this faith I intend to live and die.
Amen.

Morning Offering

O Jesus, through the Immaculate Heart of Mary,
I offer you my prayers, works, joys, and sufferings of this day
for all the intentions of your Sacred Heart,
in union with the Holy Sacrifice of the Mass throughout the world,
for the salvation of souls,
the reparation for sins,
the reunion of all Christians,
and in particular for the intentions of the Holy Father this month.
Amen.

Grace before Meals

Bless us, O Lord, and these thy gifts,
which we are about to receive from thy bounty.
through Christ our Lord. Amen.

Grace after Meals

We give thee thanks, for all thy gifts, Almighty God,
who live and reign forever.
[And may the souls of the faithful departed, through the mercy of God, rest in peace.]
Amen.

An Act of Hope

O Lord God, I hope by your grace
for the pardon of all my sins
and after life here to gain eternal happiness because you have promised it
who are infinitely powerful, faithful, kind, and merciful.
In this hope I intend to live and die.
Amen.

An Act of Love

O Lord God, I love you above all things
and I love my neighbor for your sake
because you are the highest, infinite and perfect good,
worthy of all my love.
In this love I intend to live and die.
Amen.